WHEN FAITH FEELS HEAVY

A DEVOTIONAL FOR WOMEN LEARNING TO TRUST GOD WITHOUT PRESSURE

S.T. WRIGHT

CONTENTS

This book is dedicated

to the women who kept showing up —

even when faith felt quiet,

even when strength ran thin,

even when returning felt harder than leaving.

You were never weak.

You were becoming.

AUTHOR'S NOTE

I want to say something clearly before you read any further.

I am not a preacher.

I am not a theologian.

And I did not go to seminary.

What you'll find in these pages is not a set of rules, a formula for perfect faith, or a collection of polished answers. This book was written from lived experience — from seasons of loving God deeply while still feeling tired, overwhelmed, uncertain, and human.

Everything here comes from my personal walk with God, my time in Scripture, and the slow, sometimes messy process of learning how to return to Him without shame or pressure. I'm doing my best to be honest, thoughtful, and faithful — not flawless.

I believe God often uses ordinary, imperfect people to start meaningful conversations, offer comfort, and remind us of truth. Not because we have everything figured out, but because we're willing to show up honestly.

This devotional isn't meant to replace Scripture. It's meant to sit beside it — to encourage reflection, create space, and invite you back into relationship with God at your own pace. Some Scripture passages are referenced or partially quoted to encourage you to open your Bible and spend time with them more fully if you choose.

If at any point you feel seen, less alone, or gently reminded that you don't have to get everything right to walk with God — then this book has done what it was meant to do.

You don't need to rush.

You don't need to perform.

You don't need to pretend.

Just keep returning.

— **S.T. Wright**

PART I

WHEN FAITH FEELS QUIET

Faith doesn't usually disappear all at once.
It fades quietly — through exhaustion, disappointment, unanswered prayers, and seasons that demand more than we have to give. Not because we stop believing in God, but because life keeps happening and we don't always know how to carry faith alongside it.
This part of the book is for the woman who still believes, but feels distant.
For the one who hasn't walked away — just stopped expecting closeness.
For the one who wonders why faith feels harder now than it used to.
You're not broken.
You're not failing.
And you're not alone.
Before anything can be rebuilt, there has to be permission — permission to admit where you are without fear, shame, or pressure to perform.
This is where that permission begins.

1

WHEN FAITH GOES SILENT

"The Lord is close to the brokenhearted; he rescues those whose spirits are crushed."

— PSALM 34:18

There are seasons our faith doesn't disappear — it just gets quiet.
Not loud enough to guide us.

Not strong enough to interrupt us.

Not close enough to comfort us.

Just... quiet.

Most of us don't wake up one day and decide to ignore God. Drift doesn't usually happen through rebellion. It happens through accumulation. A missed prayer here. A rushed morning there. A Sunday was skipped because we were tired. A Bible left unopened because we didn't want to deal with conviction, or because we told ourselves we'd "get back to it later."

Later has a way of stretching.

Before long, we look up and realize we haven't truly talked to God in weeks. Or months. And the distance feels confusing, because it wasn't intentional. Life just kept moving, and somewhere along the way, our awareness of God's presence faded into the background.

If that's you, let me say something you need to hear before anything else:

You are not the only one.

And God has not left you.

When faith goes quiet, the enemy loves to whisper the opposite. He'll tell you that you're alone. That you're failing. That you're not a "real Christian." That God must be disappointed by how inconsistent you've been. That other people seem to hear God clearly because they're doing something you're not.

Because if shame can isolate you, it can keep you from returning.

But Scripture tells a very different story.

Spiritual drift is part of the human experience. The Bible is full of people who loved God deeply and still experienced seasons of distance, confusion, and silence. David cried out, asking why God felt far away. Elijah, after witnessing miracles, sat under a tree, convinced he was finished and alone. Peter denied Jesus outright. Thomas doubted openly.

Drift didn't disqualify them.

It became part of their testimony.

Where we often get stuck is here: when our faith goes quiet, we assume God goes quiet too. As if His presence depends on our consistency. As if His nearness fluctuates with our performance. As if silence must mean abandonment.

But that isn't biblical truth — it's emotional interpretation.

James 4:8 says, *"Draw near to God, and He will draw near to you."*

Notice what the verse does **not** say.

It doesn't say, "After you fix yourself."

It doesn't say, "Once you've been consistent again."

It doesn't say, "If you haven't messed up too badly."

It simply says, " Draw near.

God isn't hiding. He isn't testing your worthiness. He isn't withholding himself to teach you a lesson. He's waiting — not with crossed arms, but with open ones.

So why do we stop drawing near?

For some of us, life just gets heavy. Grief changes us. Stress distracts us. Responsibilities multiply. For others, disappointment makes us numb. We prayed for something that didn't happen. We trusted God and still got hurt. And without realizing it, we pulled back — not out of anger, but out of self-protection.

And sometimes, if we're honest, sin dulls our spiritual ears. Not in a dramatic way. Slowly. Comfortably. We begin to tolerate things that make us less sensitive to God's voice, and over time, the quiet feels safer than the conviction.

That doesn't make you the villain.

It makes you human.

Psalm 34:18 says, *"The Lord is close to the brokenhearted and saves those who are crushed in spirit."*

Not "close to the perfect."

Not "close to consistent."

Close to the broken.

If your faith feels quiet right now, it doesn't mean God has stopped speaking. It means there may be layers sitting between you and His voice — distraction, disappointment, discouragement, self-reliance, unresolved hurt.

This chapter isn't here to shame you for that.

It's here to help you recognize it.

Because spiritual hearing isn't mystical or reserved for the super-holy. It's relational. It's built through proximity, not performance. God's voice becomes clearer the closer we draw — not because He was silent before, but because we're finally near enough to listen again.

Deuteronomy 31:8 says, *"The Lord himself goes before you and will be with you; he will never leave you nor forsake you."*

That promise doesn't expire during quiet seasons.

It doesn't weaken when faith feels thin.

It doesn't depend on how connected you feel.

So if you feel awkward around God right now — unsure how to pray, unsure what to say, unsure if you're even doing it "right" — you are exactly who this chapter was written for.

You're not too far.

You're not disqualified.

You're not forgotten.

Your faith is quiet — not gone.

And quiet things can be stirred again.

∾

Scriptures for Reflection

Psalm 34:18
James 4:8
Deuteronomy 31:8

Questions for Journaling

- When did my faith begin to feel quieter?
- What contributed to my drift — busyness, disappointment, grief, sin, or numbness?
- In what ways have I pulled back emotionally or spiritually, even without realizing it?

Simple Prayer

"God, I feel distant from You — but I want to draw near. I don't want to pretend or perform. I just want to hear You again. Gently stir my heart and help me come back honestly. In Jesus' name, Amen."

2

THE LIES THAT KEEP US AWAY

"You will know the truth, and the truth will set you free."

— JOHN 8:32

D rift rarely ends with distance alone.

After faith goes quiet, something else usually steps in to fill the silence. Not chaos. Not rebellion. Something much quieter and more convincing.

Lies.

They don't announce themselves as lies. They don't sound dramatic or obviously wrong. They sound reasonable. Familiar. Protective. They slip into the quiet spaces where prayer used to live and start explaining *why* it's okay that you haven't gone back yet.

Most women don't avoid God because they don't want Him.

They avoid Him because they've started believing something about Him — or about themselves — that isn't true.

And once those beliefs take root, distance stops feeling accidental. It starts feeling safer.

When Distance Turns Into Avoidance

There's a difference between drifting and staying gone.

Drifting happens without intention. Life gets busy. Pain goes unresolved. Faith fades into the background while you're managing everything else. One day, you realize you're far, and you're not even sure how it happened.

But staying away is different.

Staying away happens when something convinces you it's better not to return yet. That it would be uncomfortable. Awkward. Heavy. Exposing.

So you avoid prayer because you don't know what you'd say.

You avoid Scripture because it reminds you of what you haven't been doing.

You tell yourself you'll come back once you feel more focused, more sincere, more worthy.

Avoidance often looks calm on the outside.

Inside, it's exhausting.

And underneath it all isn't disobedience — it's belief.

Lie #1: "I'm Too Far Gone"

This lie usually shows up quietly, after enough time has passed.

It tells you that you waited too long. That you should have come back sooner. That the distance has grown into something permanent. That God might have been patient once, but surely not forever.

So instead of returning, you hesitate.

Scripture speaks directly to this fear. In Romans 8:1, we're told:

"So now there is no condemnation for those who belong to Christ Jesus."

No condemnation doesn't come with conditions.

No expiration date.

No fine print.

Belonging doesn't dissolve with distance. You don't slowly lose your place with God because you struggled, stalled, or stayed silent longer than you meant to.

Feeling far does not mean you *are* far.

Lie #2: "God Is Disappointed in Me"

This lie hits especially hard for women who are used to carrying responsibility.

You show up. You follow through. You hold things together. And when your faith feels inconsistent, you assume God must be holding you to the same standard of performance you hold yourself to.

But Psalm 103 offers a different picture:

> "He does not punish us for all our sins; he does not deal
> harshly with us, as we deserve."

> — PSALM 103:10

God sees your exhaustion before He sees your inconsistency.

Correction may come — because love corrects — but disappointment is not His posture toward you. He is not standing back with crossed arms, waiting for you to do better. He is attentive, aware, and patient.

The belief that God is disappointed often says more about how *we* speak to ourselves than how God speaks to us.

Lie #3: "I Should Fix Myself First"

This lie sounds mature. Responsible. Even spiritual.

It tells you to deal with your mess before you bring it to God. That you should get your habits back in order, your thoughts under control, your emotions settled — and *then* return.

But Scripture never requires self-repair for grace.

Through Isaiah, God says:

> *"Come now, let's settle this," says the Lord. "Though your sins are like scarlet, I will make them as white as snow."*

> — ISAIAH 1:18

The invitation is not "fix yourself."

The invitation is "come."

Healing happens in God's presence — not outside of it. Waiting until you feel ready only keeps you stuck in the very place grace was meant to meet you.

Lie #4: "I Missed My Chance"

This lie feeds on regret.

It convinces you that you ignored too many nudges. That you hesitated too long. That the moment passed and won't come back around.

But Scripture repeatedly shows a God who invites again and again.

God does not withdraw because you hesitated.

He waits.

Distance does not close the door.

It only delays the moment you walk back through it.

Lie #5: "I Don't Hear God Anymore"

This lie equates silence with separation.

But silence often means your heart is overwhelmed — not abandoned.

God is not a God of confusion. And just because His voice feels quieter does not mean He has stopped speaking. Sometimes the noise around us has simply grown louder than His whisper. Sometimes exhaustion dulls our ability to listen. Sometimes fear makes us avoid stillness.

Lack of clarity does not mean lack of presence.

Where These Lies Come From

Jesus is very clear about the source of lies.

The enemy doesn't need to convince you to stop believing in God — he only needs to keep you disconnected from Him. Lies thrive in isolation. They grow stronger the longer they go unspoken. Truth, on the other hand, invites a relationship.

When lies stay hidden, they shape decisions.

When they're exposed, they lose power.

When Truth Begins to Replace Lies

Truth doesn't shame you back into God's presence.

It invites you gently.

Truth sounds like:

God already knows.

God is still here.

You don't have to earn your way back.

Grace meets you where you are.

When truth replaces lies, distance begins to close — not all at once, but honestly.

For the Woman Carrying Quiet Guilt

Many women carry spiritual guilt silently.

You still function. You still show up for everyone else. But inside, you feel unqualified to come back. Like you've lost the right to approach God with confidence.

God is not asking you to perform.

He is asking you to come honestly.

Shame thrives in hiding.

Grace grows in honesty.

What Changes When Lies Lose Their Grip

When lies begin to loosen:

Prayer feels possible again.

Scripture feels accessible.

Guilt stops dominating.

Faith begins to breathe.

You don't need a dramatic return.

You need an honest one.

~

Reflection Questions

- Which lie feels most familiar to me right now?
- When did I start believing it?
- How has it kept me distant from God?
- What truth does Scripture offer instead?
- What would honesty with God look like today?

Prayer

God,

I confess that I've believed things about You — and about myself — that aren't true.

Help me recognize the lies that keep me distant.

Replace shame with truth and fear with trust.

I don't want to return perfectly.

I want to return honestly.

Meet me here.

Amen.

3

GOD NEVER MOVES

"I am the Lord, and I do not change."

— MALACHI 3:6

One of the most painful realizations for a woman who has drifted from God is the quiet fear that He may have moved on without her.

You don't usually say that fear out loud.

You might not even fully admit it to yourself.

But you feel it.

You wonder if God is still as close as He once was — or if the distance you feel has settled into something permanent. You question whether your inconsistency changed His posture toward you. And sometimes, without realizing it, you begin to approach God cautiously... as if you're not sure you're still welcome.

That hesitation doesn't come from rebellion.

It comes from uncertainty.

And Scripture answers that uncertainty clearly:

God never moves.

WE DRIFT — GOD DOES NOT

Distance in your faith does not happen because God steps away.

It happens because life pulls your attention elsewhere.

Responsibilities pile up. Emotional weight increases. Disappointment settles in. Exhaustion takes over. You move into survival mode. You still believe. You still love God. But you stop resting in His presence. You start functioning without noticing how far you've drifted internally.

The distance feels real.

But the source of the distance matters.

God has not gone anywhere.

That distinction is important because when you believe God moved, returning feels intimidating. When you realize *you* drifted, returning becomes possible.

GOD'S CHARACTER IS CONSISTENCY

One of the hardest things for us to trust — especially as women who carry responsibility — is consistency. People change. Relationships shift. Support disappears. So when faith feels unstable, we assume God must be unpredictable too.

But Scripture tells a different story.

In Malachi 3:6, God says:

"I am the Lord, and I do not change."

That means God's faithfulness does not depend on your performance. His nearness does not fluctuate with your consistency. Your awareness of Him may rise and fall — but His presence does not.

You may feel distant.

God is not.

THE PRODIGAL FATHER NEVER MOVED HOUSES

One of the clearest pictures of this truth is found in the story of the prodigal son.

The son left.

The father stayed.

The father didn't chase him down with punishment.

He didn't lock the door.

He didn't move away.

He watched.

He waited.

And when the son returned, the father ran toward him.

That detail matters.

The father didn't hesitate. He didn't interrogate. He didn't demand explanations. He moved toward his child because his heart never left.

Jesus tells that story on purpose.

God's posture toward you is the same.

Why Distance Feels So Personal

For many women, spiritual distance feels relational — almost like rejection.

You're used to measuring closeness through conversation, connection, and emotional presence. So when faith feels quiet, you assume something has changed between you and God.

But God's closeness is not measured by feelings.

It's measured by promises.

Hebrews 13:8 tells us:

> *"Jesus Christ is the same yesterday, today, and forever."*

The same God who met you before is still here now — unchanged, unbothered by time, and unmoved by your inconsistency.

God Pursues — He Does Not Punish

Many women confuse God's pursuit with punishment.

Conviction feels uncomfortable, so we interpret it as rejection. Correction feels exposing, so we assume disappointment. Silence feels heavy, so we assume abandonment.

But Scripture consistently shows a God who moves toward His children, not away from them.

God corrects to restore.

He convicts to heal.

He draws close to guide.

Distance does not make Him withdraw.

It invites Him to pursue.

Why This Truth Matters for Exhausted Women

When you're tired, everything feels heavier.

Guilt feels heavier.

Distance feels deeper.

Silence feels louder.

And exhaustion convinces you that reconnecting with God will require energy you don't have.

But the truth that God never moves removes pressure.

You're not trying to find Him.

You're responding to Him.

You're not rebuilding from nothing.

You're returning to something steady.

God Is Not Keeping Score

God is not tallying missed prayers.

He is not counting inconsistent days.

He is not waiting for you to prove yourself.

Scripture describes God as patient, compassionate, and slow to anger.

That means your return does not need to be impressive.

It needs to be honest.

What It Means to Come Back to a God Who Never Left

If God never moved, then returning is not about distance.

It's about attention.

It's about turning your heart back toward the One who has been present all along.

That might look like whispering a short prayer instead of a long one.

Opening Scripture without pressure to "feel something."

Acknowledging God quietly in the middle of your day.

Letting go of the belief that closeness must be earned.

Returning does not require a dramatic moment.

It requires willingness.

For the Woman Who Feels Afraid to Reconnect

If part of you feels hesitant to lean back into God, that fear makes sense.

You may be afraid of disappointment.

Of conviction.

Of being asked to change.

Of feeling exposed.

But God's nearness is not meant to overwhelm you.

It's meant to steady you.

God does not rush you.

He meets you where you are.

Truth That Grounds You

When faith feels uncertain, anchor yourself in what does not change:

God's character.
God's promises.
God's presence.
You may feel distant.
But God has not moved.

~

Reflection Questions

1. When did I begin to believe God might be distant from me?
2. What assumptions have I made about God's posture toward me?
3. How does knowing God never moves change how I approach Him?
4. Where have I confused conviction with rejection?
5. What would returning look like if I believed God was still close?

Prayer

God,

When my faith feels uncertain, remind me that You are steady.

When I feel distant, help me remember that You have not moved.

Release the fear that keeps me hesitant, and help me turn back toward You with trust.

Thank You for being faithful even when I am not.

Meet me here.

Amen.

4

WHEN DISTRACTION
REPLACES DEVOTION

"You are worried and upset over all these details... There is
only one thing worth being concerned about."

— LUKE 10:41–42

Most women don't wake up one day and decide to stop seeking God.

It happens quietly.

Devotion doesn't disappear because you stop believing. It gets crowded out by everything else demanding your attention. And because distraction feels normal — even responsible — it often goes unnoticed for a long time.

You're still functioning.

Still showing up.

Still handling what needs to be handled.

But somewhere underneath the movement, your inner life feels thinner than it used to. Less anchored. Less spacious. Less attentive.

And that quiet thinning can be hard to name, because nothing is technically "wrong."

WHY DISTRACTION IS SO EFFECTIVE

Distraction rarely feels sinful.

It feels practical.

Necessary.

Responsible.

You're answering messages. Checking schedules. Scrolling for a break. Filling every spare moment with something that keeps you moving forward. None of those things are bad on their own. Most of them are part of modern life.

The problem isn't that life is full.

The problem is that God slowly stops being centered.

Faith doesn't disappear — it gets pushed to the margins. Prayer becomes something you think about doing instead of something you do. God becomes someone you believe in, but don't actively notice.

And because distraction doesn't feel dramatic, it's easy to miss.

BUSY IS NOT THE SAME AS FULFILLED

Many women confuse busyness with purpose.

You're productive. Needed. Reliable. People count on you. And on the surface, that feels meaningful. But deep down, something feels slightly off — like you're moving a lot without being nourished.

Busyness can become a way to avoid stillness. And stillness is often where God speaks most clearly.

Scripture says:

"Be still, and know that I am God."

— PSALM 46:10

Stillness isn't inactivity.

It's attentiveness.

And attentiveness can feel uncomfortable when you've been carrying a lot. Slowing down means noticing what you've been pushing aside — fatigue, disappointment, unanswered questions, emotions you didn't have time to feel.

So instead of stillness, many of us stay busy.

WHEN SILENCE FEELS HARDER THAN NOISE

Silence is difficult when your life has been loud.

When you finally pause, thoughts surface. Emotions rise up. Questions you've avoided come forward. So instead of sitting with God, it's easier to reach for something that fills the space.

Your phone.

Background noise.

Constant input.

Distractions that numb rather than heal.

Distraction becomes a coping mechanism.

Not because you don't love God, but because you're tired. And tired people often choose what feels easiest, not what feels deepest.

How Modern Life Trains Us to Stay Spiritually Noisy

We live in a world designed to divide attention.

Notifications. Algorithms. Endless content. Constant comparison. Without realizing it, we train our minds to stay stimulated and avoid quiet.

But devotion requires presence.

And presence requires intention.

If your mind feels scattered when you try to pray, that doesn't mean you're failing. It means you've been trained to live distracted — and retraining takes patience.

When Self-Reliance Replaces God-Reliance

Another subtle shift happens when distraction increases: self-reliance.

You stop pausing to ask God because you've learned how to handle things on your own. You problem-solve. You manage crises. You push through.

Gradually, prayer becomes optional instead of essential.

Scripture gently re-centers us here:

> "Seek the Kingdom of God above all else, and live righteously,
> and he will give you everything you need."

> — MATTHEW 6:33

Seeking first doesn't mean adding God to an already full list.

It means allowing Him to be the reference point from which everything else flows.

When Good Things Become Substitutes

Distraction isn't always about bad habits.

Sometimes it's about good things taking first place — family, work, responsibility, even ministry. But good things become substitutes when they replace intimacy with God.

Jeremiah describes this exchange clearly:

> "My people have done two evil things: They have abandoned
> me—the fountain of living water—and they have dug for
> themselves cracked cisterns that can hold no water at all!"
>
> — JEREMIAH 2:13

When we rely on substitutes, we eventually feel empty.

Not because God has left — but because we stopped drinking from the source.

Why Distraction Feels Safer Than Devotion

Devotion requires honesty.

It means showing up without distractions. Without pretending. Without rushing. And that can feel vulnerable.

Distraction lets you avoid unanswered questions, uncomfortable emotions, and areas where God may be inviting change. So instead of leaning in, many women stay busy.

Not out of rebellion — but out of self-protection.

God Is Not Competing for Your Attention

Here's something important to remember: God is not demanding more from you.

He's inviting you back.

He isn't competing with your schedule. He isn't frustrated by your distraction. He understands the weight you carry.

But He gently calls you to remember where life actually flows from.

What Re-centering Looks Like in Real Life

Re-centering your faith doesn't require dramatic changes.

It might look like turning off the noise for a few minutes.

Acknowledging God quietly in the middle of your day.

Choosing presence over productivity for a moment.

Opening Scripture without pressure to feel something immediately.

Devotion isn't about doing more.

It's about paying attention again.

For the Woman Who Feels Too Busy for God

If you feel like you don't have time for devotion, pause for a moment.

The invitation isn't to rearrange your entire life.

It's to reorient your heart.

God doesn't need hours.

He needs willingness.

And He is patient.

Distraction Is Not Permanent

Awareness is the beginning of change.

The fact that you recognize distraction means your heart is already responding. God is not asking you to eliminate every distraction.

He's asking you to return to Him in the middle of your life — not outside of it.

~

Reflection Questions

- Where do I notice distraction showing up most in my life?
- What do I reach for when I avoid stillness?
- How has busyness affected my connection with God?
- What emotions surface when things get quiet?
- Where have I relied on myself instead of inviting God in?
- What small shift could help me re-center my attention?

Prayer

God,

I confess that distraction has replaced devotion in ways I didn't notice at first.

Help me slow down enough to hear You again.

Teach me to invite You into my real life — not a quieter version of it.

I don't want to be busy without being present.

Re-center my heart toward You.

Amen.

INTERLUDE — YOU'RE NOT IN TROUBLE

"So now there is no condemnation for those who belong to Christ Jesus."

— ROMANS 8:1

Before we go any further, I want you to pause.

Not to fix anything.

Not to decide anything.

Not to promise anything.

Just pause.

Because if you're anything like most women reading this, your instinct right now might be to brace yourself. To assume the next step is correction, effort, or change. To wonder what God is going to ask of you next — and whether you even have the capacity to give it.

So let me say this clearly, before we move on:

You are not in trouble.

You are not behind.

You are not failing at faith.

You are not disappointing God.

What you're experiencing is not rebellion.

It's exhaustion.

And exhaustion has a way of distorting everything — especially how we see ourselves, and how we assume God sees us.

Many women don't drift from God because they stop loving Him.

They drift because they've been strong for too long.

You've been the one holding things together. Anticipating everyone else's needs. Managing emotions, schedules, finances, and expectations. Being reliable. Being steady. Being the one people lean on.

And somewhere along the way, your own spiritual needs got postponed.

Not intentionally.

Not selfishly.

Just gradually.

You didn't wake up and decide to neglect your faith.

You simply ran out of margin.

When faith feels distant, there's often an unspoken pressure to *do something* about it.

To repent immediately.

To get disciplined.

To "get back on track."

To fix whatever went wrong.

But rushing yourself spiritually rarely leads to healing.

It usually leads to performance.

And performance has never been the foundation of a real relationship with God.

Before there is any talk of repentance, obedience, or rebuilding, there has to be safety. You need to know that you're welcome before you're asked to change.

Here's something that matters deeply:

You do not need to earn your return.

You don't need the right words.

You don't need the right emotions.

You don't need to feel more guilty, more motivated, or more spiritual.

You don't need to clean yourself up before coming back.

You just need honesty.

And maybe rest.

Most women try to return to God from a place of depletion.

They're tired, overwhelmed, emotionally stretched thin — yet they expect themselves to suddenly show up spiritually energized. That's not realistic. And it's not kind.

God does not invite you back so He can exhaust you further.

He invites you back so He can carry what you've been holding alone.

Before you move forward, you're allowed to stop and breathe. To admit that you're tired. To acknowledge that you don't have all the answers. To say, *"I don't know how to do this anymore."*

That isn't a weakness.

That's the beginning of trust.

If part of you feels afraid of what comes next, that makes sense.

You might be afraid God will ask too much.

Afraid he'll bring everything up at once.

Afraid returning means immediate change or sacrifice.

But God doesn't overwhelm.

He leads gently.

He moves patiently.

He meets you where you are — not where you think you should be.

You don't have to take ten steps forward.

You only need to stop running.

Let this be a moment of permission.

Permission to rest without guilt.

To be honest, without fear.

To acknowledge distance without shame.

To move slowly without pressure.

This is not the moment to evaluate your faith.

It's the moment to let yourself be seen.

And being seen doesn't require effort.

Only openness.

The next part of this book will talk about return.

But return is not a sprint.

It's not a performance.

And it's not punishment.

It's a response.

And responses come more naturally when fear is removed.

So before we go any further, sit with this truth:

You are not in trouble.

You are not late.

You are not disqualified.

You are tired.

And God knows that.

$\sim$

A Gentle Pause

If you need to, put the book down for a moment.

Breathe.

Let your shoulders relax.

You don't need to rush into the next chapter.

It will still be here when you're ready.

5

REPENTANCE WITHOUT SHAME

*"The sacrifice you desire is a broken spirit. You will not reject
a broken and repentant heart."*

— PSALM 51:17

For many women, the word *repentance* carries weight.

Not the grounding kind.

Not the freeing kind.

The heavy kind.

It brings up memories of being corrected harshly. Of being exposed before being understood. Of being told what was wrong without being shown how to heal. Repentance starts to sound like failure. Like disappointment. Like punishment.

So when faith feels distant, repentance can feel intimidating — something to avoid rather than embrace.

But repentance was never meant to shame you.

It was meant to bring you home.

Why Repentance Feels So Heavy

Most women don't resist repentance because they don't want to change.

They resist it because they associate it with condemnation.

Somewhere along the way, repentance became tied to:

- focusing on everything you did wrong
- reliving mistakes you've already punished yourself for
- feeling worse before feeling better
- proving you're sorry enough

That version of repentance is exhausting.

And it's not biblical.

When repentance is framed as humiliation instead of restoration, it stops feeling safe. And when something doesn't feel safe, we avoid it — not because we're rebellious, but because we're protecting ourselves.

What Repentance Actually Is

At its core, repentance simply means to *turn*.

To change direction.

To realign.

To come back.

Repentance is not groveling.

It is not self-punishment.

It is not earning forgiveness.

Repentance is a response to grace — not a prerequisite for it.

Psalm 103 describes God this way:

> *"The Lord is compassionate and merciful, slow to get angry*
> *and filled with unfailing love."*

— PSALM 103:8

A God who is slow to anger is not waiting to crush you when you return.

He's waiting to restore you.

SHAME AND CONVICTION ARE NOT THE SAME

This distinction matters more than most of us realize.

Shame sounds like:

"You are bad."
"You should have known better."
"You don't deserve closeness."
Conviction sounds like:
"This isn't who you are."
"There's a better way."
"Come back."

Shame pushes you away from God.

Conviction draws you toward Him.

If what you feel makes you want to hide, withdraw, or disappear spiritually, that is not coming from God. God does not use shame to bring His children home.

Why Women Carry Extra Weight Here

Women tend to internalize responsibility deeply.

You don't just regret mistakes — you carry them. You replay them. You analyze them. You wonder how things might have been different if you'd done better.

So when repentance comes up, it can feel overwhelming. Like one more thing you're failing at. Like another reminder that you didn't do enough, try hard enough, or stay consistent enough.

But repentance was never meant to be another burden.

It's meant to release one.

You Don't Repent to Be Accepted

This truth changes everything.

You do not repent so that God will accept you.

You repent because you already are.

Romans 5:8 reminds us:

> *"God showed his great love for us by sending Christ to die for us while we were still sinners."*

Grace came first.

Acceptance came first.

Love came first.

Repentance follows grace — not the other way around.

Repentance Is Rarely a Single Moment

Another misconception is that repentance must be dramatic or complete.

That you need to confess everything all at once.

That you need perfect clarity.

That you need to feel deeply emotional or spiritually intense.

But repentance is often gentle and gradual.

Sometimes it looks like admitting you're tired.

Sometimes it looks like acknowledging you've been distant.

Sometimes it's simply saying, "God, I need help."

That counts.

God honors honesty more than performance.

What Repentance Looks Like in Real Life

For exhausted women, repentance doesn't usually look like hours spent on your knees.

It looks like a quiet moment of truth.

Like releasing control.

Like letting go of self-reliance.

Like choosing to stop running emotionally.

Repentance is not fixing your life overnight.

It's turning your heart.

God Is Not Keeping You at Arm's Length

Some women hesitate to repent because they're afraid of what comes after.

Afraid God will demand immediate change.

Afraid He'll bring everything up at once.

Afraid they'll fail again.

But God doesn't overwhelm.

He restores step by step.

He doesn't drag you forward.

He walks with you.

Repentance is not about how much you change today.

It's about who you turn toward.

If You Feel Resistance Right Now

That resistance makes sense.

You might feel emotionally tired. Unsure where to start. Afraid of being exposed. Worried you'll disappoint God again.

But repentance is not about promising perfection.

It's about choosing direction.

And direction can change in a single moment.

GRACE MAKES REPENTANCE POSSIBLE

Without grace, repentance would be unbearable.

But with grace, repentance becomes freeing.

Because grace says:

You're safe.

You're loved.

You're not alone.

You're not too late.

Repentance is simply agreeing with God about what needs to shift — and trusting Him to help you shift it.

FOR THE WOMAN AFRAID TO COME HOME

If you're hesitant to repent because you don't know what it will cost you, hear this:

God is not waiting to take something from you.

He's waiting to give you rest.

He is not asking you to carry more.

He is asking you to let go.

~

Reflection Questions

1. What comes to mind when I hear the word repentance?
2. How has shame shaped my view of returning to God?
3. Where have I been afraid to be honest with Him?
4. What might repentance look like in this season of my life?
5. What am I holding onto that feels heavy?

Prayer

God,

I want to return without shame.

I confess that I've carried guilt instead of grace.

Help me see repentance as an invitation, not a punishment.

I turn my heart back toward You — not perfectly, but honestly.

Restore what feels distant and lead me gently forward.

Amen.

6

A FATHER WHO
RUNS TOWARD YOU

"While he was still a long way off, his father saw him..."

— LUKE 15:20

Many women believe God tolerates them.

They believe He forgives because He has to. That grace is extended out of obligation, not joy. That acceptance is possible, but closeness might be withheld. And when they imagine returning to Him after drifting, they don't picture open arms — they picture distance, disappointment, or restraint.

But that picture of God is not biblical.

Scripture does not present a Father who waits with crossed arms. It presents a God who moves first. A God who responds quickly. A God who restores fully.

One of the most misunderstood stories in Scripture is the parable of the prodigal son — not because it's unclear, but because we tend to focus on the wrong part.

We often focus on how far the son wandered. How reckless he was. How much he lost. How badly he failed.

But Jesus emphasizes something else entirely.

> *"While he was still a long way off, his father saw him and was filled with compassion; he ran to his son, threw his arms around him, and kissed him."*
>
> — LUKE 15:20

The father didn't wait for the son to reach the house.

He didn't demand an explanation.

He didn't require proof of repentance.

He ran.

That detail matters more than we realize, because it reveals God's heart. God responds to **direction**, not distance. The moment you turn toward Him — even hesitantly, even unsure — He moves toward you with compassion.

Many women approach God cautiously when they return.

They brace themselves emotionally. They expect correction before connection. Distance before closeness. They're prepared to be forgiven, but not fully embraced.

But Scripture shows us a different posture entirely.

> *"See what great love the Father has lavished on us, that we should be called children of God."*
>
> — 1 JOHN 3:1

God is not guarded with His children.

He is not reserved.

He is not withholding affection until trust is rebuilt.

You do not re-enter a relationship on probation.

You belong.

One of the most tender moments in the parable happens when the son begins to speak.

He has a speech prepared. He rehearsed it on the walk home. He expects to negotiate his place — to be reduced, to be humbled, to earn his way back slowly.

But the father interrupts him.

Before the son can explain, the father restores his identity.

> *"Quick! Bring the best robe and put it on him. Put a ring on his finger and sandals on his feet."*

> — LUKE 15:22

The robe, the ring, and the sandals were not decorative. They were declarations of belonging, authority, and sonship.

The father restores identity before addressing behavior.

That order is intentional.

God does not fix you before He loves you.

He loves you — and love does the fixing.

Some women struggle to receive this kind of grace because they're afraid of what it implies.

They worry it excuses past choices. That it minimizes responsibility. That it ignores growth.

But grace does not ignore growth — it fuels it.

> *"But God demonstrates his own love for us in this: While we*
> *were still sinners, Christ died for us."*

— ROMANS 5:8

Grace meets us at our lowest point and lifts us upward. It doesn't leave us where we were — it leads us forward.

The Father runs not because the Son stayed the same.

He runs because his son came home.

Another detail we often overlook is what happens next.

There is no quiet forgiveness.

There is no restrained response.

There is a celebration.

> *"For this son of mine was dead and is alive again; he was lost*
> *and is found."*

— LUKE 15:24

Heaven rejoices when a child returns.

God does not begrudgingly restore you. Your obedience does not inconvenience Him. Your return does not frustrate Him.

It delights Him.

If you've believed that God tolerates you rather than delights in you, this chapter is meant to gently dismantle that lie.

So if you are standing at the edge of return — unsure how God will respond — let this truth steady you.

God runs toward His children.

He does not hesitate.

He does not delay.

He does not shame.

You are not met with distance.

You are met with open arms.

～

Reflection Questions

- How do I imagine God responding when I return to Him?
- What fears do I carry about being fully welcomed back?
- What would change if I truly believed God runs toward me?

Prayer

Father,

Help me see You as You truly are.

Remove the fear that keeps me hesitant and guarded.

Teach me to receive Your love without bracing myself for disappointment.

I step toward You — trusting Your heart.

Amen.

PART II

REBUILDING GENTLY

After you admit that faith feels quiet, something usually follows.
A quiet question.
What now?
Not in a dramatic way — but in a tired one.
You don't want to walk away from God.
But you also don't want to force something that feels fragile.
This part of the book is not about fixing your faith.
It's about rebuilding trust — slowly, realistically, and without pressure.
Here, we talk about renewing your mind when your thoughts feel loud.
About obedience that doesn't exhaust you.
About community that supports instead of overwhelms.
About purpose that grows out of pain instead of pretending it didn't happen.
Rebuilding doesn't happen through intensity.
It happens through consistency, grace, and honesty.
This part is about learning how to stay — gently.

7

RENEWING YOUR MIND

"Let God transform you into a new person by changing the way you think."

— ROMANS 12:2

For many women, faith doesn't fall apart first in their actions. It falls apart in their thoughts.

You can love God deeply and still feel trapped in mental loops — overthinking conversations, replaying mistakes, anticipating worst-case scenarios, quietly believing things about yourself that you'd never say out loud to anyone else. And the hardest part is that it can all happen while you're still "doing life."

You're still showing up. Still working. Still being responsible. Still being the one everyone counts on.

But inside, your mind is loud.

And when your mind is loud, faith can feel far — not because God is distant, but because your thoughts are constantly speaking over Him.

Renewing your mind sounds spiritual.

But in real life, it often feels exhausting.

Especially when you're already tired.

The Mental Load Women Carry

Most women are carrying on a constant internal dialogue.

It sounds like: *Did I forget something?*

What if this goes wrong?

I should be doing more.

Why can't I get it together?

Everyone else seems to handle this better.

And it doesn't turn off when the house gets quiet. It follows you into bed. It shows up in the middle of prayer. It colors how you hear God — if you hear Him at all.

Because when your mind is overwhelmed, prayer doesn't feel like rest.

It feels like one more place your thoughts show up to accuse you.

Why Renewing Your Mind Feels So Hard

Renewing your mind isn't difficult because you don't want change.

It's difficult because your thought patterns feel automatic. You don't sit down and choose them like a menu. They just arrive — and sometimes they arrive faster than you can catch them.

And when you're exhausted, the thoughts get even louder.

You start thinking faster. Assuming the worst. Reacting more emotionally. Bracing before anything even happens. Not because you're dramatic — because your nervous system is tired and your heart is trying to protect you.

A lot of women assume renewing your mind means "thinking positively."

But Scripture never asks you to pretend.

It invites you to notice... and then redirect.

Gently. Intentionally. Over time.

WHAT RENEWING YOUR MIND ACTUALLY MEANS

Let's look at Scripture together.

In Romans chapter 12, verse 2, it says:

> *"Don't copy the behavior and customs of this world, but let God transform you into a new person by changing the way you think."*

> — ROMANS 12:2

Notice what that verse is saying.

It doesn't say: "Transform yourself by trying harder."

It says: *let God transform you* — and one of the ways He does that is by changing how you think.

So renewing your mind isn't about self-improvement.

It's about letting God meet you inside the place you've been battling alone.

Because God knows something we forget: your thought life shapes your peace.

Your Thoughts Quietly Shape Your Direction

Unchecked thoughts don't just make you feel something.

They steer you.

If you constantly think *I'm failing*, you live discouraged.

If you constantly think *I can't rest*, you stay exhausted.

If you constantly think *God expects more*, you end up avoiding Him.

If you constantly think *I'll never change*, you stop trying.

And then your faith becomes filtered through the same voice that's been pressuring you all along.

This is why renewing your mind isn't optional for spiritual growth.

It's essential.

Because God isn't only concerned with what you do.

He cares about what's forming you.

"Take Every Thought Captive" (Without Beating Yourself Up)

Many women feel guilty about their thoughts.

They assume that having anxious, critical, fearful thoughts means something is wrong with their faith.

But Scripture doesn't say, "Never have a wrong thought."

It shows us what to do when wrong thoughts show up.

In 2 Corinthians 10:5, it talks about taking thoughts captive — meaning thoughts will come. The goal isn't perfection. It's awareness.

Renewal begins when you pause long enough to notice what's

running through your mind — without judging yourself for having a human brain.

Sometimes the most spiritual moment isn't a beautiful prayer.

It's noticing the sentence you keep repeating in your head and finally saying:

Wait... is that even true?

WHY GRACE HAS TO BE PART OF THIS

If you try to renew your mind through pressure, you will quit.

Because pressure leads to self-criticism. Discouragement. The feeling that you're failing even at healing.

But grace keeps you engaged.

Grace says: *Let's look at this honestly.*

Grace says: *Let's replace this gently.*

Grace says, "Let's try again."

God is not impatient with your mind.

He knows how long you've been thinking this way. He knows what you've lived through. He knows why certain thoughts formed in the first place.

And He is not disgusted by the process.

He is present in it.

What Renewal Looks Like in Everyday Life

Renewing your mind does not require hours of quiet time and perfect concentration.

It often looks like:

- pausing a thought spiral mid-sentence
- questioning a familiar lie
- choosing truth over self-blame
- letting God interrupt your inner narrative

Sometimes renewal is simply saying:

That thought doesn't align with the truth.
That's fear talking.
That's shame talking.
That's not God's voice.

And letting it pass without obeying it.

This is where a lot of women get stuck: we assume we have to *stop* the thought completely before we're "doing it right."

But often, the win is smaller and quieter:

You notice it sooner than you used to.

You spiral for ten minutes instead of two hours.

You come back to peace a little faster.

That's renewal.

Replacing Lies With Truth (Without Overload)

You don't need to memorize dozens of verses overnight.

You need a few anchors — the kind you can reach for in the moment.

When your mind says: *I'm not enough,*

What God is showing you is that your worth was never something you earned — it was given.

When your mind says: *I should be further along,*

What God is showing you is that growth takes time, and He is not rushing you.

When your mind says: *God must be tired of me,*

What God is showing you — again and again in Scripture — is that He is patient, compassionate, and steady.

Renewal happens one replacement at a time.

One thought. One truth. One gentle redirect.

Why Exhaustion Makes Renewal Slower (and That's Not Failure)

When you're tired, your mind defaults to survival.

You assume worst-case scenarios faster. You get more reactive. You feel more sensitive. You have less emotional margin.

That doesn't mean you're failing.

It means you're human.

And renewing your mind during exhaustion requires extra gentleness — not extra pressure.

God knows this season of your life.

He is not asking for perfection.

He is offering support.

For the Woman Who Feels Mentally Stuck

If you feel trapped in your thoughts, hear this:

You are not broken.

You are not beyond renewal.

You are not failing at faith.

You are learning how to think differently.

And that takes time.

God is not disappointed in the process.

He is present in it.

Small Steps Still Count

Renewal doesn't happen all at once.

It happens when you:

notice one thought,

choose one truth,

pause one spiral,

extend yourself one moment of grace.

Those small moments add up.

That is how God rebuilds peace — slowly, faithfully, gently.

~

Reflection Questions

- What thoughts do I notice repeating most often?
- Which thoughts feel rooted in fear or shame?
- How do these thoughts affect my emotions and faith?
- What truth could gently replace them this week?
- What would progress — not perfection — look like for me?

Prayer

God, my mind feels busy and heavy.

Help me notice the thoughts that pull me away from peace.

Teach me how to replace fear with truth — gently and patiently.

I don't want to think perfectly.

I want to think with You.

Renew my mind one step at a time.

Amen.

8

DAILY HABITS OF OBEDIENCE

"If you love me, obey my commandments."

— JOHN 14:15

For many women, the word *obedience* feels heavier than it should. It can sound like rules.

Like discipline.

Like one more area where you're falling short.

And when you're already tired mentally, emotionally, or spiritually, the idea of "daily obedience" can feel overwhelming before you even start.

But obedience was never meant to exhaust you.

It was meant to anchor you.

Why Obedience Gets Misunderstood

A lot of us learned obedience as something rigid.

Do this.

Don't do that.

Try harder.

Be more disciplined.

But Scripture shows us something different.

In John 14:15, Jesus says that obedience flows out of love, not pressure. What He's showing us here is that obedience isn't about forcing behavior. It's about relationship. When love is present, obedience follows naturally.

That changes everything.

Obedience Is Not About Doing More

One of the biggest lies women believe is that obedience means taking on more spiritual tasks on an already full plate.

But obedience is not about doing more for God.

It's about responding to God.

Sometimes obedience looks like action.

Sometimes it looks like rest.

Sometimes it looks like surrender.

And sometimes it looks like stopping.

Scripture reminds us, *"It is good to wait quietly for the salvation of the Lord."* (Lamentations 3:26)

. . .

What God is teaching us here is that obedience sometimes means slowing down instead of speeding up.

Stillness can be obedience.

Small Habits Matter More Than Big Moments

We often think spiritual growth comes from big breakthroughs.

But Scripture points us to something quieter.

In Luke 16:10, we're reminded that faithfulness in small things matters. God is showing us that daily obedience is built in ordinary moments—not dramatic ones.

Obedience grows in:

short prayers whispered under your breath

choosing honesty over avoidance

pausing before reacting

letting God into your thoughts

asking for help instead of pushing through alone

These moments may feel small.

Heaven does not see them that way.

Prayer That Fits Real Life

Prayer doesn't need to sound polished.

It needs to be real.

Scripture invites us to *"pour out your hearts to Him, for God is our refuge."* (Psalm 62:8)

What this tells us is that prayer doesn't require perfect words—it requires honesty.

For exhausted women, prayer often looks like:

"God, I'm tired."
"I don't know what to do."
"Please help me today."
"I need You right now."
Those prayers count.

Listening Instead of Forcing

Many women struggle to hear God because they're trying too hard.

They assume obedience means figuring everything out.

But Scripture often shows God speaking in whispers, not demands.

In 1 Kings 19, God wasn't in the wind or the fire. He was in the gentle whisper. What God is teaching us here is that listening requires space, not striving.

Obedience often begins with paying attention—not pushing harder.

Surrender Is a Daily Choice

Surrender sounds spiritual, but it's deeply practical.

Jesus models this in Luke 22:42, when He prays, *"Not my will, but yours be done."* What we learn here is that surrender doesn't mean you're weak—it means you trust God more than your own control.

Surrender looks like:

releasing outcomes
admitting when you're overwhelmed
letting go of expectations
choosing trust over certainty

And it usually happens in the same areas repeatedly.

That's normal.

Why Obedience Feels Different in Hard Seasons

Not every season requires the same pace.

In Ecclesiastes 3, Scripture reminds us that there is a time for everything. God is showing us that obedience adjusts with the season you're in.

There are seasons for building.

Seasons for resting.

Seasons for healing.

Seasons for waiting.

God is not asking you to run when you're barely standing.

He's asking you to lean on Him.

Creating Space Instead of Adding Pressure

Fasting and discipline are often misunderstood.

They aren't about punishment.

They're about making room.

In Matthew 6, Jesus talks about practicing spiritual habits quietly and intentionally—not for performance. What God is showing us here is that obedience is personal, not performative.

Sometimes obedience looks like removing distractions instead of adding obligations.

Obedience Is Built Through Relationship

You don't obey a distant God.

You obey someone you trust.

And trust grows slowly through consistency, honesty, grace, and patience.

In Proverbs 3:5–6, we're reminded that trusting God with our paths brings direction. What this shows us is that obedience deepens as relationship deepens—not through pressure.

Let Obedience Be Gentle

If obedience feels heavy, something is off.

Because obedience was never meant to crush you.

It was meant to steady you.

God is not asking you to carry more weight.

He's inviting you to let Him help carry what you already have.

~

Reflection Questions

How have I defined obedience in the past?

Where have I confused obedience with pressure?

What small habit feels realistic right now?

Where might God be inviting me to slow down?

What does surrender look like in this season?

How can prayer fit into my real life?

What distractions might I need to let go of?

What step of obedience feels gentle—not forced?

Prayer

God, help me see obedience as a relationship, not pressure.

Show me the small steps that matter in this season.

Teach me how to listen, surrender, and trust each day.

Meet me in my real life, exactly where I am. Amen.

9

COMMUNITY & ACCOUNTABILITY

"Two people are better off than one..."

— ECCLESIASTES 4:9–10

Most women don't struggle because they don't love God. They struggle because they're trying to carry everything alone.

At first, isolation doesn't feel dangerous.

It feels normal.

Necessary, even.

You handle what needs to be handled. You keep going. You show up. And over time, doing it alone starts to feel like the only option, not because it's healthy, but because it's familiar.

THE LIE THAT STRENGTH MEANS DOING IT ALONE

Many women learn early on that being strong means being independent.

You manage it.

You don't complain.

You don't ask for help.

From the outside, you look capable.

From the inside, you're exhausted.

And slowly, without realizing it, you begin to believe that needing support means you're weak or failing. But Scripture never equates isolation with strength. In fact, it consistently points us in the opposite direction.

GOD NEVER DESIGNED YOU TO WALK ALONE

All the way back at the beginning, God makes something clear.

"It is not good for the man to be alone." (Genesis 2:18)

What God is showing us here is important: even in a perfect world, before sin or brokenness entered the picture, isolation was not part of His design. Community wasn't added later as a fix — it was foundational from the start.

You were never meant to carry life by yourself.

Why Isolation Feels Safer (But Isn't)

Isolation can feel safer because it removes risk.

No one can judge you.

No one sees your struggle.

No one asks hard questions.

For women who carry emotional responsibility, whether as wives, mothers, daughters, or simply the "strong one," isolation can slowly become an identity.

But isolation doesn't actually protect you.

It drains you.

What feels like self-preservation often turns into quiet burnout.

Accountability Is About Support, Not Control

The word *accountability* can sound intimidating.

It often carries images of being monitored, corrected, or exposed.

But biblical accountability looks very different.

"Two people are better off than one, for they can help each other succeed. If one person falls, the other can reach out and help." (Ecclesiastes 4:9–10)

Notice what's emphasized here: help, not punishment. Accountability exists so that when you fall — and everyone does — someone is there to reach out, not point fingers.

Why Women Avoid Community

Many women avoid community not because they don't value it, but because they've been hurt before. Others don't want to burden anyone. Some feel misunderstood. Many believe they *should* be able to handle things on their own.

But Scripture gently challenges that belief.

"Without wise leadership, a nation falls; there is safety in having many advisers." (Proverbs 11:14)

What God is teaching us here is simple: seeking support isn't weakness — it's wisdom. You weren't meant to figure faith, healing, or life alone.

Community Looks Different in Different Seasons

Community doesn't always mean a large group or structured setting. Sometimes it's one trusted friend. A mentor. A prayer partner. Someone who checks in consistently.

> *"As iron sharpens iron, so a friend sharpens a friend."*
>
> — PROVERBS 27:17

Growth happens through proximity, trust, and shared honesty, not pressure.

Why Accountability Helps Faith Stay Alive

When faith feels distant, isolation makes drifting easier. No one notices. No one asks. No one reminds you of the truth when your own voice feels tired.

That's why Scripture urges us not to withdraw from one another.

> *"Let us think of ways to motivate one another to acts of love and good works."*
>
> — HEBREWS 10:24–25

Encouragement isn't optional. It's protective.

Healing Requires Safe Connection

Scripture is clear about this:

> *"Confess your sins to each other and pray for each other so that you may be healed."*
>
> — JAMES 5:16

Healing doesn't come from exposing everything to everyone. It comes from letting the *right* people into the places where you've been hiding.

Secrecy keeps wounds open.

Safe connection allows healing to begin.

You Don't Have to Share Everything

Accountability is not oversharing.

It's appropriate sharing.

God often brings one or two safe people, not a crowd. Trust builds slowly. That's okay. You are allowed to move at a pace that feels safe.

When Community Feels Hard to Find

If community feels distant right now, Scripture still offers hope.

"God places the lonely in families."

— PSALM 68:6

God sees isolation — and He responds to it. Community may not look like what you expected, but it will be intentional. You are not overlooked.

For the Woman Who Feels Alone Right Now

If you feel alone in your faith, hear this clearly:

You are not weak for needing support.

You are not failing because you're tired.

You were never meant to carry this alone.

God often meets us through people: gently, quietly, and patiently.

LET COMMUNITY BE GENTLE

Community does not need to be overwhelming.

Start small.

Start safe.

Start honest.

God is not asking you to expose everything.

He's inviting you to stop being alone.

~

Reflection Questions

- Where have I been carrying things alone?
- What fears do I have about community?
- Who feels emotionally safe in my life?
- Where might God be inviting me to reach out?
- How has isolation affected my faith?
- What would support — not pressure — look like?
- What small step toward connection feels possible right now?

Prayer

God, I confess that I've tried to carry too much alone.

Help me let go of the belief that strength means isolation.

Show me safe people who can walk with me.

Teach me how to receive support with grace.

I trust You to meet me through connection. Amen.

10

PURPOSE AFTER PAIN

"He comforts us in all our troubles so that we can comfort others."

— 2 CORINTHIANS 1:4

P ain has a way of making everything feel pointless.

When you've been through loss, disappointment, betrayal, burnout, or seasons that didn't turn out the way you prayed, purpose can feel like a cruel concept. Something meant for other people. People whose lives stayed intact. People who didn't detour.

And yet—this is where Scripture speaks with the most honesty.

Because God never promises a pain-free life.

But He does promise that pain is not wasted.

When Pain Disrupts the Story You Planned

Most women don't grieve just what happened.

They grieve what *didn't*.

The marriage that didn't turn out the way you hoped.

The family dynamics that never healed.

The child who struggles.

The business that didn't grow the way you envisioned.

The season that took more from you than it gave.

Pain interrupts the narrative you were living by.

And when that happens, purpose can feel lost—not because it's gone, but because it no longer looks the way you expected.

God Does Not Waste Pain

This is not a comforting phrase unless it's actually true.

Scripture doesn't minimize suffering—but it does give it meaning.

In Romans 8:28, it says:

> *"God causes everything to work together for the good of those who love God and are called according to his purpose for them."*

What God is showing us here is not that everything *is* good—but that He is capable of weaving even the hardest parts of your story into something redemptive.

Pain is not proof that God has left.

It's often the place where purpose deepens.

Purpose Is Not Always a Platform

One of the biggest misconceptions about purpose is that it must be big, visible, or impressive.

But Scripture shows us that purpose often unfolds quietly.

Through character.

Through compassion.

Through resilience.

Through empathy you didn't have before.

Pain has a way of softening places in you that comfort never touches.

That softness becomes a place where God can work.

What If Your Pain Changed You—for the Better?

Not in a cliché way.

Not in a forced "everything happens for a reason" way.

But in a grounded, honest way.

Pain often teaches you:

How to sit with others who are hurting

How to listen instead of fix

How to extend grace

How to let go of control

How to depend on God differently

Those things shape purpose—even when you don't realize it yet.

God Works Through What Broke You

Scripture is full of people whose purpose emerged *after* pain.

Joseph was betrayed.

Moses was rejected.

David was pursued.

Ruth lost everything.

Peter failed publicly.

None of them stepped into purpose without first walking through something that broke them open.

In 2 Corinthians 1:3–4, it says:

> *"He comforts us in all our troubles so that we can comfort others."*

What God is showing us here is that comfort received becomes comfort given. Your pain doesn't disqualify you—it equips you.

Purpose Grows in Process, Not Pressure

Many women feel pressure to "do something meaningful" with their pain.

But purpose doesn't require urgency.

God doesn't rush healing.

He doesn't force lessons.

He doesn't demand productivity from your wounds.

Purpose unfolds as you heal—not before.

Sometimes the most purposeful thing you can do is rest.

You Are Not Behind

If your life doesn't look like you expected by now, hear this clearly:

You are not behind.

You are not late.

You are not off track.

God is not bound by your timeline.

In Psalm 66:12, Scripture says God brings people through fire and flood—but leads them to a place of abundance. What God is showing us is that hard seasons are not the destination.

They are part of the journey.

Purpose Can Look Like Faithfulness

Purpose doesn't always look like doing more.

Sometimes it looks like:

staying soft when bitterness would be easier

choosing hope when cynicism feels safer

showing up again after disappointment

trusting God when answers are slow

Those choices matter more than you think.

For the Woman Who Feels Disoriented

If pain has left you unsure of who you are or where you're going, you're not failing.

You're becoming.

God often quietly rebuilds purpose—layer by layer—through surrender, honesty, and trust.

You don't need to figure it all out today.

You just need to keep walking with Him.

God Writes the Story Forward

Pain may have marked your past—but it does not define your future.

God is still writing.

Still redeeming.

Still restoring.

In Isaiah 61, Scripture speaks of beauty rising from ashes. What God is telling us here is that what was burned is not the end of the story.

It's the beginning of something transformed.

Let Purpose Be Gentle Too

Purpose doesn't have to be heavy.

It can be lived quietly.

Faithfully.

Honestly.

God is not asking you to turn your pain into a performance.

He's inviting you to let Him bring meaning out of it—at the pace of healing.

~

Reflection Questions

Where has pain disrupted my expectations?

What have I learned about myself through hardship?

How has pain softened or changed me?

Where do I see God sustaining me, even quietly?

What pressure do I feel about "finding purpose"?

What would it look like to release that pressure?

How might God be working through my story?

What step of faith feels possible right now?

Prayer

God, I bring You the parts of my story that still hurt.

Help me trust that nothing I've walked through is wasted.

Show me a purpose that fits this season—not pressure.

Heal what needs healing and redeem what feels broken.

I trust You to write my story forward. Amen.

INTERLUDE — WHEN THE STRUGGLE IS WITHIN

What looks like peace on the outside can still be a war on the inside.

You can stand in a room full of people and assume everyone is doing fine, yet behind calm faces are private struggles, unspoken worries, temptations, and heavy thoughts that are hard to explain.

Many of those struggles are not only emotional or circumstantial. They are spiritual.

Every believer has a fight. And many days, that fight is not with other people — it is within.

Scripture puts words to this experience.

> *"For the flesh desires what is contrary to the Spirit, and the Spirit what is contrary to the flesh. They are in conflict with each other, so that you are not to do whatever you want."*

> — GALATIANS 5:17

There are moments when your spirit longs for God — for prayer, for the Word, for obedience, for purity. And at the very same time, your

87

natural desires pull you toward comfort, distraction, pride, anger, or avoidance. You may plan to pray and suddenly feel exhausted. You may open your Bible and feel restless. You may want to forgive, but your mind replays the hurt instead.

This tension is real.

And feeling it does not make you weak or strange — it makes you human.

Even the apostle Paul described this inner conflict, where he desired what was right yet felt another force pulling him toward sin. The struggle is not an excuse to remain stuck, but it is a reminder that the battle is understood — and that God has already given a way forward.

The question becomes: how do you live faithfully in a body that still has appetites, habits, and weaknesses?

Scripture does not pretend this is easy.

> *"Those who belong to Christ Jesus have crucified the flesh with its passions and desires. Since we live by the Spirit, let us also walk by the Spirit."*
>
> — GALATIANS 5:24–25

Crucifixion is not comfortable language. It was slow. It was painful. And it was final. When the Bible uses this image, it is teaching us that denying the flesh is not about willpower or perfection — it is about choosing life over what feels easy but leads us away from Christ.

This does not mean pretending the struggle does not exist. It means acknowledging it honestly and choosing obedience anyway.

Paul echoes this call when he writes, *"Present your bodies as a living sacrifice, holy and pleasing to God... be transformed by the renewing of your mind."* (Romans 12:1–2)

A living sacrifice is still alive — which means it can try to crawl off the altar. That is why surrender is not a one-time moment. It is daily. Sometimes hourly. Sometimes minute by minute.

Part of crucifying the flesh also means recognizing what feeds it. Some battles remain strong because they are constantly being nourished. Some temptations stay loud because they are continually given attention.

Jesus warned His disciples with both compassion and wisdom:

> *"Watch and pray so that you will not fall into temptation. The spirit is willing, but the flesh is weak."*
>
> — MATTHEW 26:41

Watching means paying attention to what opens doors.

Praying means admitting you cannot win spiritual battles with natural strength alone.

And when you do stumble — because everyone does — do not run from God in shame. Run to Him in honesty.

> *"If we confess our sins, He is faithful and just to forgive us and to cleanse us from all unrighteousness."*
>
> — 1 JOHN 1:9

Confession is not humiliation. It is healing.

God is not looking for flawless performance. He is forming sons and daughters who keep returning, keep yielding, and keep walking forward.

A mind ruled by the flesh fixates on comfort, pleasure, and approval in the moment. But a renewed mind begins to look upward.

"Set your minds on things above, not on earthly things."

— COLOSSIANS 3:1–2

This does not mean escaping responsibility on earth — it means refusing to let temporary desires rule your heart.

So today, choose the Spirit again.

"Walk by the Spirit, and you will not gratify the desires of the flesh."

— GALATIANS 5:16

Walking is step by step. Choosing prayer when you do not feel like it. Choosing the Word when distraction calls. Choosing forgiveness when bitterness wants to stay. Choosing holiness when sin looks easier.

And as you walk, the Spirit strengthens you. He reshapes your desires. He teaches you how to live as someone who belongs to Jesus.

The things of the flesh promise comfort but leave emptiness. They promise pleasure but leave regret. They promise control but create bondage.

But what you surrender to Christ bears fruit.

What you place on the altar makes room for true life.

So keep walking. Keep yielding. Keep returning.

Victory is not only possible — it is part of your inheritance in Christ.

~

Reflection

Where do you feel the tension between what your spirit desires and what your flesh resists?

What might God be inviting you to surrender again — not in shame, but in trust?

Prayer

Jesus, You know me fully. You see where I am strong, and You see where I am tired. Today, I ask You to strengthen my spirit. Help me choose You when obedience feels difficult and comfort feels easier. Teach me to walk by Your Spirit, one step at a time. Amen.

PART III

STAYING WHEN IT'S HARD

At some point, the struggle changes.

You're not questioning faith anymore — you're tired of starting over.

Tired of falling, returning, and wondering if real change is actually possible.

Tired of managing yourself instead of living freely.

This part of the book is for the moments when faith isn't dramatic — it's stubborn.

When returning doesn't feel inspiring, it just feels necessary.

When trust feels unsafe.

When control feels easier than surrender.

When consistency matters more than emotion.

This is where faith becomes less about feeling close to God.

and more about choosing to stay connected — even imperfectly.

Not because you're strong.

But because God is steady.

This is where endurance grows.

This is where grace deepens.

This is where a God-led life becomes real.

11

CONSISTENCY OVER EMOTION

"Let us not become weary in doing good..."

— GALATIANS 6:9

L et's just say the quiet part out loud.

Most women don't struggle with faith because they don't believe in God.

They struggle because their emotions are all over the place.

Some days you feel steady. Hopeful. Grounded.

Other days, you wake up already irritated, discouraged, tired, or numb — and nothing specific even happened. You just feel *off*.

And when that keeps happening, you start asking yourself questions you don't really want to answer.

What's wrong with me?

Why can't I stay consistent?

Why does my faith feel strong one day and shaky the next?

If that sounds familiar, I want you to hear this first:

You're not broken.

You're not failing.

And you're not doing faith "wrong."

You're just human — living in a body, in a season, carrying more than most people see.

When Your Feelings Feel Like the Most Honest Voice

Emotions feel convincing because they're immediate.

They respond to everything:

lack of sleep, stress, hormones, conflict, grief, overstimulation, mental overload.

And for women especially, emotions rarely show up alone. They pile on top of each other.

You're not just tired — you're tired *and* needed.

You're not just overwhelmed — you're overwhelmed *and* responsible.

You're not just discouraged — you're discouraged *and* expected to keep going.

So when your faith starts to feel inconsistent, it makes sense that you blame yourself.

But the problem isn't your faith.

It's that your emotions have been doing a job they were never meant to do.

The Emotional Whiplash No One Talks About

A lot of women live in emotional whiplash.

You wake up with good intentions.

You plan to pray.

You plan to be patient.

You plan to stay grounded.

And then life happens.

Someone needs you immediately.

Plans change.

A conversation drains you.

Something doesn't go as expected.

You absorb someone else's stress.

By the end of the day, you feel disconnected — not because you stopped loving God, but because you ran out of emotional bandwidth.

That doesn't mean you drifted spiritually.

It means you lived a real day in a demanding season.

Why Faith Based on Emotion Burns You Out

Here's where many women get stuck.

Without realizing it, they build their faith around how they *feel*.

They think:

"I'll pray when I feel inspired."
"I'll read Scripture when it speaks to me."
"I'll trust God when I feel peaceful."

But life doesn't always cooperate with inspiration.

And when faith depends on emotion, you stop showing up the moment it feels dry, uncomfortable, or quiet. Eventually, consistency starts to feel like pressure, and pressure turns into guilt.

That's how burnout sneaks in.

Not because God demands too much — but because emotions were never meant to lead your faith.

What Consistency Actually Is (Because It's Not What You Think)

Let's clear something up.

Consistency does not mean:

never missing a day
always feeling motivated
being spiritually disciplined at all times
doing the same thing in every season

Consistency simply means returning.

Returning when you drift.

Returning when prayer feels awkward.

Returning when you feel numb.

Returning when emotions are messy.

Consistency isn't intensity.

It's persistence.

Scripture reminds us in *Galatians 6:9* not to grow weary in doing good, because growth comes in time. What God is really showing us there is this: faith grows slowly. Quietly. Repetitively. Not through emotional highs, but through steady presence.

Why Consistency Feels Boring (and Why That's Not a Bad Thing)

If we're honest, consistency doesn't feel exciting.

It looks like showing up when nothing feels different.

Choosing trust without emotional reassurance.

Staying connected without any immediate payoff.

And that can feel deeply unsatisfying if you're used to measuring growth by how something feels.

But consistency builds something emotion never can.

It builds stability.

And stability is what holds you when emotions swing.

Consistency in Motherhood and Caregiving

If you're a mother or caregiver, emotional consistency can feel almost impossible.

You may feel overstimulated, touched out, resentful — and then guilty for feeling that way. You might feel spiritually disconnected simply because you're depleted.

Some days, faith looks like survival.

And that does not disqualify you.

Consistency in these seasons often looks like:

whispering short prayers instead of long ones

choosing patience imperfectly

returning after snapping at someone

trusting God while feeling emotionally empty

That still counts.

God does not measure your faith by how calm or spiritual you feel. He sees the faithfulness it takes to keep returning when your emotional capacity is stretched thin.

Consistency in Work, Calling, and Responsibility

If you work outside the home, run a business, or take on financial responsibility, consistency looks different, too.

You may feel discouraged when effort doesn't lead to an outcome.

You may feel frustrated when obedience doesn't feel rewarded.

You may feel spiritually dry when work consumes all your energy.

Faith in these seasons rarely feels emotional.

It feels steady.

In *Psalm 37:5*, Scripture invites us to commit our way to the Lord and trust Him to act. What that shows us is that commitment comes before clarity — and trust often grows without emotional reinforcement.

When Faith Feels Quiet or Numb

Spiritual numbness is one of the most misunderstood seasons of faith.

Many women assume numbness means God is distant, or they've failed, or they're doing something wrong.

But numbness often follows grief, prolonged stress, disappointment, or burnout.

Consistency keeps the door open during these seasons.

You don't need to *feel* close to God to stay connected.

You just need to stay.

God Honors Showing Up — Even Like This

God does not require emotional enthusiasm.

He honors faithful presence.

Jesus talks in *Matthew 6* about practicing faith quietly, without performance. What God is showing us is that faith practiced without emotion still matters.

The tired days count.

The distracted days count.

The days you almost didn't show up still count.

For the Woman Who Feels Inconsistent

If you feel inconsistent, hear this clearly:

You are not unstable.

You are not weak.

You are learning endurance.

Consistency isn't about never drifting.

It's about refusing to stay gone.

Stop Waiting to Feel Ready

You don't need emotional clarity to be faithful.

You don't need motivation.

You don't need certainty.

You don't need spiritual energy.

You need willingness.

God works with willingness far more than emotion.

Let Consistency Be Gentle

Consistency doesn't mean forcing yourself into something rigid.

It means choosing to stay connected — imperfectly.

God is not asking you to feel more.

He's asking you to remain.

12

WHEN YOU FALL AGAIN

"The godly may trip seven times, but they will get up again."

— PROVERBS 24:16

I don't think anyone talks enough about how discouraging it feels to fall *after* you already decided to come back to God.

Not the first fall.

The second one.

The one that happens after you pray again.

After you felt hopeful.

After you told yourself, *This time will be different.*

Because when you fall again, it doesn't just feel like a mistake.

It feels like proof.

Proof that maybe you don't really change.

Proof that you might not be as strong as you thought.

Proof that you might always circle the same things.

And that's when the conversation in your head shifts.

The first time you drifted, you were confused. Or hurt. Or over-whelmed.

This time, you *knew better.*

And knowing better somehow makes it feel worse.

You don't even want to talk about it out loud, because it sounds embarrassing when you say it.

"I came back… and then I messed up again."

So instead of returning again, you hesitate.

You pull back.

You wait.

Not because you don't want God, but because you don't know how many times you're allowed to show up with the same mess.

I think this is where a lot of women quietly give up — not officially, not dramatically — but internally.

They still believe in God.

They still love Him.

But they stop expecting closeness.

They start managing their faith instead of living it.

They tell themselves things like:

I'll come back when I do better.

I'll pray again when I feel less fake.

I'll try again once I get myself together.

And slowly, shame does what pain couldn't do — it creates distance.

Here's the part we rarely say clearly enough:

Falling again does not mean you failed at faith.

It means you're human and still healing.

Scripture actually assumes this will happen.

That surprised me when I first noticed it.

In Proverbs 24:16, it says, *"The godly may trip seven times, but they will get up again."*

What's important isn't the number — it's the expectation.

God didn't say, "If you fall."

He said *when*.

And what He focuses on isn't the falling — it's the getting back up.

That verse alone dismantles the idea that real faith means never struggling again.

But shame doesn't quote Scripture accurately.

Shame takes moments and turns them into identity.

It whispers things like:

You always do this.
Nothing really changed.
You're wasting God's patience.

And if you're already tired — emotionally, mentally, physically — those thoughts land harder.

Especially if you're a woman who carries a lot.

If you're the one who keeps things running.

The one who absorbs emotions.

The one who thinks ahead for everyone else.

When *you* fall again, it doesn't just feel personal — it feels irresponsible.

And that weight is heavy.

There's something else I want to say gently, because I think many women need to hear it:

A lot of what we call "spiritual failure" is actually exhaustion.

It's a nervous system overload.

It's grief you didn't have time to process.

It's the resentment you weren't allowed to name.

It's a responsibility without rest.

And when your body and mind are overwhelmed, your spiritual life feels it too.

That doesn't mean you don't love God enough.

It means you're depleted.

God already knows this about you.

Psalm 103 says that the Lord is compassionate and tender, *"for He knows how weak we are; He remembers we are only dust."*

That verse doesn't excuse sin — but it reframes weakness.

God is not shocked when you struggle again.

He accounted for your humanity before you ever noticed it yourself.

One of the most damaging beliefs women carry is that growth should look clean.

That once you "get it," you shouldn't revisit the same struggles.

But healing doesn't work that way.

Growth loops.

It revisits old places with new awareness.

It exposes layers you couldn't see before.

The fact that you *notice* the fall sooner now matters.

The fact that it bothers you differently matters.

The fact that you want to return again matters.

That is growth — even if it doesn't feel victorious.

There's a verse in Micah 7:8 that says, *"Do not rejoice over me, my enemy; when I fall, I will rise."*

I love that it doesn't deny the fall.

It acknowledges it openly.

And then it refuses to let the fall have the final word.

That's resilience, not perfection.

One of the hardest moments after falling again is prayer.

You don't know what to say.

You feel repetitive.

You feel exposed.

You feel like you should come up with something better this time.

But Scripture doesn't tell us God wants polished prayers after failure.

Psalm 51 says God does not despise a broken and repentant heart.

Not a perfect one.

Not an impressive one.

An honest one.

Sometimes the bravest prayer after falling again is simply:

> *"I'm here. I don't know what to say. But I'm here."*

That still counts.

There's another misconception that keeps women stuck here:

The idea that falling again resets your progress.

It doesn't.

You are not starting from zero.

You are returning with more self-awareness, more humility, more truth than before.

Lamentations says God's mercies are new every morning — not because we erase yesterday, but because mercy meets us *inside* it.

Your past attempts still taught you something.

Your struggle still shaped you.

Your return still matters.

I think of the story Jesus tells in Luke 15 about the lost sheep.

What always stands out to me isn't how the sheep got lost — it's that the shepherd went after it.

He didn't lecture on it.

He didn't make it prove it learned its lesson.

He carried it back.

That's not a story about irresponsible sheep.

It's a story about committed love.

And that's how God responds to your return — even the hundredth time.

If you fell again, this is what I want you to hear clearly:

You are not disqualified.

You are not on probation.

You are not disappointing God.

You are learning what you need.

You are discovering your limits.

You are being invited — again — into honesty instead of performance.

James 4:8 says, *"Come close to God, and God will come close to you."*

There is no clause attached to that verse.

No limit.

No expiration.

No "unless you already messed this up too many times."

Just an invitation.

Maybe falling again isn't proof that you can't change.

Maybe it's proof that God is still patient enough to walk with you while you do.

And maybe the bravest thing you can do right now isn't promising you'll never fall again — but choosing to return anyway.

Right where you are.

13

WHEN LETTING
GO FEELS UNSAFE

"Trust in the Lord with all your heart..."

— PROVERBS 3:5

I don't think people realize how unhelpful the phrase *"just live and let God"* can be.

I know it's meant to sound freeing.

I know it's supposed to feel peaceful.

But every time I hear it, something in me tightens instead of relaxes.

Because living and letting God means not controlling things.

And not controlling things feels unsafe when control is what's kept you standing.

I don't mean that dramatically.

I mean it very literally.

I am guilty of trying to control.

Still.

It's not that I don't believe in God.

I do.

It's not that I think He's incapable.

I know He's not.

But there are places in my life where trust feels thin — not absent, just fragile. Places where letting go feels less like faith and more like exposure. And once you've learned how quickly life can change, how suddenly things can fall apart, how easily disappointment can arrive, control stops feeling like a flaw.

It starts feeling like wisdom.

I notice it most when things feel uncertain.

I don't pray more.

I think more.

I run scenarios in my head without realizing I'm doing it. I replay conversations that haven't happened yet. I prepare myself emotionally for outcomes that might never come. I brace myself for disappointment before it arrives, hoping that if I expect less, it will hurt less.

Not because I want to be pessimistic — but because being prepared feels safer than being surprised.

It's like my mind stays on alert, as if awareness itself could somehow prevent pain.

And for a while, it works.

Control keeps things contained.

Predictable.

Manageable.

Until it doesn't.

What people don't talk about enough is how exhausting control actually is.

It looks like strength from the outside.

But inside, it's constant tension.

It's never fully resting.

Never fully exhaling.

Always holding something, just in case.

And when you live that way long enough, faith starts to feel heavy — not because God is demanding, but because you're carrying things He never asked you to.

There's a verse in Proverbs that people quote often: *"Trust in the Lord with all your heart; do not depend on your own understanding."*

What gets me every time is that word *depend*.

Because I don't just use my understanding — I rely on it.

I depend on logic to keep me safe.

I depend on preparation to keep me steady.

I depend on anticipation to soften the blow of disappointment.

And what God is showing us here isn't that understanding is bad. It's that understanding that makes a terrible foundation. It wasn't designed to carry the weight we put on it, especially in seasons where answers are incomplete and outcomes are uncertain.

Control feels responsible, but it's heavy.

And the weight doesn't always show up as stress right away. Sometimes it shows up as restlessness. As irritability. As the inability to fully relax even when everything appears fine on the surface.

You can be sitting still and still feel like you're bracing.

That's not peace.

Jesus talks about this in Matthew 6 when He speaks about worry. He doesn't scold people for being anxious. He points out, very gently, that worry doesn't actually accomplish what we think it does.

He says worrying can't add a single hour to your life.

What God is showing us there is not, *"Stop worrying or else."*

It's, *"This thing you're doing to protect yourself... it isn't working."*

And sometimes realizing that — really letting that sink in — is harder than just being told what to do.

When Avoidance Feels Safer Than Trust

There's another way control shows up that we don't talk about very often.

It doesn't look like over-planning.

It doesn't look like fixing.

Sometimes it doesn't look like doing anything at all.

Sometimes control looks like avoiding.

We tend to think of procrastination as a time problem.

A discipline problem.

A motivation problem.

A laziness problem.

But most of the time, procrastination has nothing to do with time.

It has everything to do with emotion.

Think about the things you put off the longest.

It's rarely the easy stuff.

It's rarely the neutral stuff.

It's the things that bring up dread.

Fear.

Pressure.

Guilt.

The possibility of disappointment.

When you imagine doing those things, something tightens in your chest. Your body reacts before your mind even explains it.

And without realizing it, you step back.

Not because you don't care — but because caring feels heavy.

This shows up spiritually more than we want to admit.

We procrastinate prayer.

We delay obedience.

We put off opening our Bible again.

We tell ourselves we'll come back to God when we feel more ready, more focused, more sincere.

But what we're really avoiding isn't God.

We're avoiding how we think we'll feel in His presence.

Sometimes it's guilt.

Sometimes it's fear that we haven't changed enough.

Sometimes it's exhaustion from trying before and feeling like it didn't last.

Sometimes it's the quiet thought, *"What if I disappoint Him again?"*

So instead of showing up honestly, we delay.

In Romans 7, Paul describes this inner tension so clearly — wanting to do what's right, yet not doing it. Not because he didn't love God, but because something inside him resisted the weight of expectation.

What Scripture shows us is that there isn't failure.

It's humanity.

Procrastination often feels safer than trust because trust requires presence.

Avoidance keeps things at a distance.

It delays the moment when feelings surface.

It postpones vulnerability.

But distance also has a cost.

There's a line in Psalm 32 where David talks about staying silent before God — and how that silence made him feel heavy inside. What he's describing isn't punishment. It's the weight of holding things in alone.

Avoidance doesn't protect us from heaviness.

It creates it.

We don't procrastinate because we don't care.

We procrastinate because we care deeply — and we're afraid of what will happen if we engage fully.

What if I try and fail again?

What if I open my heart and feel exposed?

What if I don't hear God clearly?

What if I do hear Him — and I don't like what He says?

Those are real fears.

Especially for women who already carry so much.

When you're used to holding everything together — emotionally, mentally, relationally — stepping into trust feels like stepping into uncertainty without armor.

So instead of surrender, we stall.

We scroll.

We stay busy.

We tell ourselves we'll deal with it tomorrow.

And shame quietly grows in the delay.

Hebrews says, *"Today, if you hear His voice, do not harden your hearts."*

That verse isn't about pressure.

It's about timing.

God knows that delay doesn't soften things — it hardens them. Not because He withdraws, but because avoidance reinforces fear.

The invitation here isn't to force yourself into action.

It's to ask a gentler question:

What am I afraid of feeling if I move toward God right now?

Fear of disappointment?

Fear of silence?

Fear of being seen too clearly?

God already knows the answer.

He's not waiting for you to be braver.

He's waiting for you to be honest.

Jesus says in Matthew 11, *"Come to Me, all who are weary and burdened, and I will give you rest."*

Notice He doesn't say, *"Come once you've dealt with it."*

He doesn't say, *"Come when you've stopped procrastinating."*

He says, " Come *weary.*

Come burdened.

Come unsure.

Come hesitant.

Rest isn't the reward for obedience.

It's the starting point.

If you've been avoiding God lately, it doesn't mean you're drifting away.

It may mean you're overwhelmed by how much you care.

And God can meet you there — gently, patiently, without pressure.

Sometimes the most faithful thing you can do isn't to fix your habits or force consistency.

It's to stop running from the feelings that surface when you think about coming back.

To sit with them.

To name them.

To bring them with you instead of waiting for them to disappear.

Procrastination loses its power when shame is removed.

And shame cannot survive in the presence of grace.

You don't have to rush back to God.

But you don't have to stay away either.

Even a small step counts.

Even a quiet prayer counts.

Even opening your heart just enough to say, *"I don't know how to do this right now,"* is still movement toward Him.

And that's always enough to begin.

~

A Quiet Prayer

God,

I confess how often I try to stay in control because I'm afraid of what might happen if I let go.

I want to trust You, but sometimes fear feels louder than faith.

Help me notice when I'm gripping too tightly.

Help me loosen my hands — even just a little.

Teach me the difference between responsibility and control, between wisdom and fear.

When uncertainty makes me restless, remind me that You are already there.

When I don't know what to do next, help me stay present rather than panic.

And when I struggle to trust You fully, meet me in the honesty of that struggle.

I don't need all the answers.

I just need You.

Amen.

14

WHEN YOU FALL AGAIN

"Though I fall, I will rise."

— MICAH 7:8

There's a particular kind of discouragement that doesn't come from the first failure.

It comes from the second one.

Or the third.

Or the moment you realize you've circled back to the same struggle you thought you were past.

That's the moment that feels hardest to bring to God — not because you don't believe He's good, but because you're tired of apologizing for the same thing. Tired of starting over. Tired of wondering whether grace still applies when progress feels slow.

Falling again doesn't just hurt.

It embarrasses.

And embarrassment has a way of convincing us to stay quiet.

. . .

Most people don't walk away from God in one dramatic decision. They drift. They try. They recommit. They fall short. They promise to do better. And somewhere along the way, the cycle itself becomes the reason they stop showing up.

Not because they don't want God, but because they don't want to disappoint Him again.

That's the lie.

One of the most subtle tactics the enemy uses isn't temptation.

It's discouragement after failure.

He doesn't need you to stop believing in God.

He just needs you to believe that *you* are the problem.

That God's patience must eventually run out.

That grace has an expiration date.

That repeated weakness disqualifies you.

But Scripture tells a very different story.

In Proverbs, it says, *"The godly may trip seven times, but they will get up again."*

Not *if* they fall.

When.

God is not surprised by repetition. He is not shocked by how long it takes for growth to occur. And He is not measuring your faith by how clean your record looks.

What God watches is whether you come back.

. . .

One of the most damaging things we do after falling again is that we delay our return.

We tell ourselves we need time.

We need to get it together.

We need to feel more sincere before praying again.

But distance doesn't heal shame — it deepens it.

The longer we stay away, the louder the accusations get.

Peter knew this feeling well.

He didn't just fail quietly. He denied Jesus publicly — three times — after insisting he never would. His failure was loud, visible, and undeniable. And when it happened, Scripture says he wept bitterly.

Not because he didn't love Jesus.

But because he did.

And yet, when Jesus rose from the dead, He didn't avoid Peter.

He went looking for him.

In John 21, Jesus meets Peter on the shore. He doesn't confront him aggressively. He doesn't lecture him. He doesn't list his mistakes.

He asks one question – three times.

"Do you love Me?"

What Jesus was doing wasn't reopening Peter's failure. He was restoring Peter's identity.

Each question met a denial.

Each answer rebuilt trust.

Each moment reminded Peter that failure didn't cancel calling.

That's how God works.

Falling again doesn't erase what God has already done in you.

It doesn't reset you to zero.

Growth is not linear. Faith is not fragile. And obedience is not a performance measured by perfection.

God is far more patient with the process than we are.

The shame that follows repeated failure often sounds reasonable.

It tells you:

"You should be further along by now."

"If your faith was stronger, this wouldn't keep happening."

"You're wasting God's time."

But Romans tells us clearly: *"There is now no condemnation for those who are in Christ Jesus."*

Not *less* condemnation.

None.

What God removes, we don't get to reapply.

One of the reasons falling again feels so devastating is that we confuse conviction with condemnation.

Conviction draws you closer.

Condemnation pushes you away.

Conviction says, "Come back."

Condemnation says, "Stay hidden."

God corrects with clarity and love. Shame confuses, isolates, and paralyzes.

If what you're feeling makes you want to disappear, it's not coming from Him.

There's something deeply humbling about realizing that willpower alone isn't enough.

That growth requires dependence.

That strength is something you receive, not manufacture.

Paul talks about this when he says God's power is made perfect in weakness.

Not in success.

Not in control.

In weakness.

Which means your struggle doesn't disqualify you from God's presence — it often becomes the place where His presence is most real.

Falling again can feel like proof that you haven't changed.

But sometimes it's actually proof that you're aware now in ways you weren't before.

Awareness hurts.

Growth is uncomfortable.

Healing exposes what needs attention.

And God is not rushing you through that process.

There's a story in Scripture where a man asks Jesus to heal his son. Jesus tells him that anything is possible if he believes. And the man responds honestly:

"I do believe — help me overcome my unbelief."

That prayer isn't polished.

It isn't confident.

But it's real.

And Jesus responds to it.

God honors honesty far more than appearances.

When you fall again, the invitation isn't to quit.

It's to come closer.

To stop trying to prove you're worthy of grace and start receiving it instead.

Grace was never a reward for improvement.

It was always a gift for the willing.

You don't need to punish yourself to show God you're serious.

You don't need to withdraw to earn your way back.

You don't need to wait until you "feel ready."

God meets you in the moment you turn back — not the moment you get it right.

Micah writes, *"Though I fall, I will rise. Though I sit in darkness, the Lord will be my light."*

Notice the confidence there.

Not in behavior.

In God.

That's the difference.

If you've fallen again, you're not failing at faith.

You're practicing returning.

And returning — again and again — is the heart of a God-led life.

$$\sim$$

A Prayer for When You've Fallen Again

God,

I'm tired of apologizing for the same things.

I'm tired of wondering if You're disappointed in me.

I'm tired of feeling like I should be further along by now.

But I don't want to stay distant.

I don't want to hide.

And I don't want shame to have the final word.

Help me come back — not in fear, but in trust.

Remind me that Your grace isn't fragile and Your patience isn't limited.

Teach me how to rise again without punishing myself.

I'm here.

I'm willing.

And I trust that You are still with me.

Amen.

15

LIVING A GOD-LED LIFE

"What does the Lord require of you? To do what is right, to love mercy, and to walk humbly with your God."

— MICAH 6:8

For a long time, I thought living a God-led life meant reaching some kind of arrival point.

A place where faith felt natural.

Where obedience didn't feel like resistance.

Where trust came easily, and doubt stayed quiet.

I thought one day I'd wake up and feel *aligned.*

Settled.

Certain.

But that version of faith never really came.

What did come was something quieter — and far more honest.

A God-led life isn't a life without struggle.

It's a life where struggle doesn't have the final word.

It's not about doing everything right or hearing God clearly all the time. It's about learning to stay open even when clarity doesn't come quickly. About choosing relationship over performance. Presence over perfection.

Living God-led doesn't mean you stop wrestling.

It means you stop walking away when the wrestling begins.

Some days, living God-led looks steady.

Prayer feels natural.

Scripture feels alive.

Trust feels possible.

Other days, it looks very ordinary.

It looks like choosing not to numb out.

Like pausing instead of reacting.

Like catching yourself before control takes over — and gently releasing it again.

It looks like returning.

Again and again.

Scripture describes this kind of life simply.

In Micah 6:8, we're told that God asks us *to do what is right, to love mercy, and to walk humbly with Him.*

What stands out to me is the word *walk.*

Not run.

Not perform.

Not prove.

Walk.

Slow.

Intentional.

Daily.

A God-led life is not built in dramatic moments. It's formed in quiet ones — the small decisions no one else sees. The moments where you choose honesty instead of hiding. Trust instead of control. Obedience instead of delay.

Living God-led doesn't mean you won't make mistakes.

It means you won't let mistakes convince you that you no longer belong with God.

Failure doesn't end the relationship.

Distance does — and distance often happens slowly, one hesitation at a time.

God is never the one pulling away.

One of the most freeing realizations in my faith has been this:

God is not asking me to be impressive.

He's asking me to be willing.

Willing to listen.

Willing to respond.

Willing to admit when I'm afraid.

Willing to come back when I fall.

That's it.

Jesus never invited people into a system.

He invited them into a way of life.

"Follow Me."

Not "get it right first."

Not "fix yourself."

Not "figure everything out."

Follow.

That invitation still stands.

A God-led life doesn't mean every decision feels clear.

Sometimes you won't know if you're moving in obedience or simply doing the best you can with what you know. Sometimes you'll pray and still feel unsure. Sometimes you'll step forward without peace—and find it only after you move.

God is not limited by your uncertainty.

He is patient with your learning.

Here's what living God-led often looks like in real life:

- choosing to pause when you want to react
- praying honestly instead of perfectly
- asking for help instead of pushing through alone
- showing up even when you feel emotionally empty
- releasing outcomes you can't control
- returning quickly instead of disappearing in shame

None of that is dramatic.

But it's deeply faithful.

If you've been waiting to feel ready before fully surrendering, I want to gently tell you this:

Readiness rarely comes first.

Willingness does.

God meets you in motion, not mastery.

There will be seasons where your faith feels strong.

And seasons where it feels thin.

Neither disqualifies you.

Faith is not measured by consistency of feeling — but by consistency of return. And every time you return, something deepens.

Living God-led doesn't mean God controls your life like a script.

It means you learn to trust His character when the script is unclear.

It means choosing relationship over explanation.

It means believing that even when you don't understand the path, you are still held on it.

You don't need to become someone else to live this way.

You don't need a different personality, a different past, or a cleaner story.

God is not asking you to erase who you are.

He is inviting you to walk with Him as you are — honest, learning, imperfect, and still deeply loved.

If you've drifted before, you can return again.

If you've fallen before, you can rise again.

If you've struggled with control, fear, avoidance, or shame — you are not behind.

You are human.

And God is not finished.

A God-led life is not loud.

It's steady.

It's built one decision at a time, one prayer at a time, one moment of honesty at a time. It doesn't demand perfection.

It asks for presence.

If this book has done anything, I hope it's reminded you of this:

You don't have to have everything figured out to walk with God.

You just have to keep walking.

~

A Final Prayer

God,

I don't want to live ahead of You or apart from You.

I want to walk with You — even when the path feels unclear.

Teach me how to listen without fear, obey without pressure, and trust without needing control.

Help me return quickly when I drift and rise gently when I fall.

I don't need to be perfect.

I just want to be present.

Lead me — one step at a time.

Amen.

A CLOSING NOTE

If you take nothing else from this book, I hope you take this:

You are not behind.

Not in your faith.

Not in your healing.

Not in your life.

If your journey with God has felt messy, inconsistent, quiet, or slower than you expected, that does not mean it has been wrong. It means it has been human.

Faith was never meant to be lived perfectly.

It was meant to be lived honestly.

You don't need to remember every insight from these pages.

You don't need to apply everything at once.

You don't need to walk away feeling inspired, energized, or certain.

If all this book did was remind you that you are still welcome with God — exactly as you are — then it has done its job.

You will drift sometimes.

You will struggle sometimes.

You will fall and return more times than you can count.

That is not failure.

That is a relationship.

God is not measuring your faith by consistency of feeling, clarity of direction, or visible progress. He is present in the returning. He meets you in the honesty. He walks with you in the becoming.

So take this with you:

Return when you're tired.

Return when you're unsure.

Return when you don't have the words.

Return when all you can offer is willingness.

You don't have to rush.

You don't have to perform.

You don't have to figure everything out.

Just keep walking.

God is already there.

www.ingramcontent.com/pod-product-compliance
Lightning Source LLC
Chambersburg PA
CBHW032038040426
42449CB00007B/933